THIS JOURNAL BELONGS TO:

_____

_____

DATE	RISK MANAGEMENT
	◯ 1-2% of Your Portfolio
	◯ Liquidity

TICKER

ENTRY

Execution Price	Where Did You Find The Trade	Purchase Date

WHY

What Indicators Confirmed The Trade

EXIT

Stop Loss Price Level	Profit Target

WHY

Reason Sold	Date Sold

NOTES

DATE	RISK MANAGEMENT
	○ 1-2% of Your Portfolio
	○ Liquidity

TICKER

ENTRY

Execution Price	Where Did You Find The Trade	Purchase Date

WHY

What Indicators Confirmed The Trade

EXIT

Stop Loss Price Level	Profit Target

WHY

Reason Sold	Date Sold

NOTES

	DATE	RISK MANAGEMENT
		◯ 1-2% of Your Portfolio
		◯ Liquidity

TICKER

ENTRY	Execution Price	Where Did You Find The Trade	Purchase Date
WHY	What Indicators Confirmed The Trade		
EXIT	Stop Loss Price Level		Profit Target
WHY	Reason Sold		Date Sold

NOTES

	DATE	**RISK MANAGEMENT**
		○ 1-2% of Your Portfolio ○ Liquidity

TICKER			
ENTRY	Execution Price	Where Did You Find The Trade	Purchase Date
WHY	What Indicators Confirmed The Trade		
EXIT	Stop Loss Price Level		Profit Target
WHY	Reason Sold		Date Sold

NOTES

DATE	RISK MANAGEMENT
	◯ 1-2% of Your Portfolio
	◯ Liquidity

TICKER

ENTRY

Execution Price	Where Did You Find The Trade	Purchase Date

WHY

What Indicators Confirmed The Trade

EXIT

Stop Loss Price Level	Profit Target

WHY

Reason Sold	Date Sold

NOTES

_____
_____
_____
_____
_____
_____
_____
_____
_____

	DATE	RISK MANAGEMENT
		◯ 1-2% of Your Portfolio
		◯ Liquidity

TICKER

ENTRY	Execution Price	Where Did You Find The Trade	Purchase Date
WHY	What Indicators Confirmed The Trade		
EXIT	Stop Loss Price Level		Profit Target
WHY	Reason Sold		Date Sold

NOTES

_____
_____
_____
_____
_____
_____
_____
_____
_____

DATE	RISK MANAGEMENT
	◯ 1-2% of Your Portfolio
	◯ Liquidity

TICKER

ENTRY	Execution Price	Where Did You Find The Trade	Purchase Date

WHY	What Indicators Confirmed The Trade

EXIT	Stop Loss Price Level	Profit Target

WHY	Reason Sold	Date Sold

NOTES

	DATE	**RISK MANAGEMENT**
		◯ 1-2% of Your Portfolio
		◯ Liquidity

TICKER

ENTRY	Execution Price	Where Did You Find The Trade	Purchase Date
WHY	What Indicators Confirmed The Trade		
EXIT	Stop Loss Price Level	Profit Target	
WHY	Reason Sold	Date Sold	

NOTES

	DATE	**RISK MANAGEMENT**
		◯ 1-2% of Your Portfolio
		◯ Liquidity

TICKER

ENTRY	Execution Price	Where Did You Find The Trade	Purchase Date
WHY	What Indicators Confirmed The Trade		
EXIT	Stop Loss Price Level		Profit Target
WHY	Reason Sold		Date Sold

NOTES

DATE	**RISK MANAGEMENT** ○ 1-2% of Your Portfolio ○ Liquidity

TICKER			
ENTRY	Execution Price	Where Did You Find The Trade	Purchase Date
WHY	What Indicators Confirmed The Trade		
EXIT	Stop Loss Price Level	Profit Target	
WHY	Reason Sold	Date Sold	

NOTES

	DATE	**RISK MANAGEMENT**
		○ 1-2% of Your Portfolio
		○ Liquidity

TICKER

ENTRY	Execution Price	Where Did You Find The Trade	Purchase Date

WHY	What Indicators Confirmed The Trade

EXIT	Stop Loss Price Level	Profit Target

WHY	Reason Sold	Date Sold

NOTES

DATE	RISK MANAGEMENT
	○ 1-2% of Your Portfolio
	○ Liquidity

TICKER

ENTRY	Execution Price	Where Did You Find The Trade	Purchase Date
WHY	What Indicators Confirmed The Trade		
EXIT	Stop Loss Price Level	Profit Target	
WHY	Reason Sold	Date Sold	

NOTES

DATE	RISK MANAGEMENT
	◯ 1-2% of Your Portfolio
	◯ Liquidity

TICKER

ENTRY

Execution Price	Where Did You Find The Trade	Purchase Date

WHY

What Indicators Confirmed The Trade

EXIT

Stop Loss Price Level	Profit Target

WHY

Reason Sold	Date Sold

NOTES

DATE	RISK MANAGEMENT
	◯ 1-2% of Your Portfolio
	◯ Liquidity

TICKER

ENTRY	Execution Price	Where Did You Find The Trade	Purchase Date
WHY	What Indicators Confirmed The Trade		
EXIT	Stop Loss Price Level	Profit Target	
WHY	Reason Sold	Date Sold	

NOTES

	DATE	**RISK MANAGEMENT**
		○ 1-2% of Your Portfolio
		○ Liquidity

TICKER

ENTRY	Execution Price	Where Did You Find The Trade	Purchase Date
WHY	What Indicators Confirmed The Trade		
EXIT	Stop Loss Price Level		Profit Target
WHY	Reason Sold		Date Sold

NOTES

DATE	RISK MANAGEMENT
	◯ 1-2% of Your Portfolio
	◯ Liquidity

TICKER

ENTRY

Execution Price	Where Did You Find The Trade	Purchase Date

WHY

What Indicators Confirmed The Trade

EXIT

Stop Loss Price Level	Profit Target

WHY

Reason Sold	Date Sold

NOTES

DATE		**RISK MANAGEMENT**
		◯ 1-2% of Your Portfolio
		◯ Liquidity

TICKER

ENTRY	Execution Price	Where Did You Find The Trade	Purchase Date
WHY	What Indicators Confirmed The Trade		
EXIT	Stop Loss Price Level	Profit Target	
WHY	Reason Sold	Date Sold	

NOTES

	DATE	**RISK MANAGEMENT**
		○ 1-2% of Your Portfolio
		○ Liquidity

TICKER			
ENTRY	Execution Price	Where Did You Find The Trade	Purchase Date
WHY	What Indicators Confirmed The Trade		
EXIT	Stop Loss Price Level		Profit Target
WHY	Reason Sold		Date Sold

NOTES

	DATE	**RISK MANAGEMENT**
		○ 1-2% of Your Portfolio
		○ Liquidity

TICKER

ENTRY	Execution Price	Where Did You Find The Trade	Purchase Date
WHY	What Indicators Confirmed The Trade		
EXIT	Stop Loss Price Level	Profit Target	
WHY	Reason Sold	Date Sold	

NOTES

_____
_____
_____
_____
_____
_____
_____
_____
_____
_____

	DATE	**RISK MANAGEMENT**
		◯ 1-2% of Your Portfolio
		◯ Liquidity

TICKER			
ENTRY	Execution Price	Where Did You Find The Trade	Purchase Date
WHY	What Indicators Confirmed The Trade		
EXIT	Stop Loss Price Level	Profit Target	
WHY	Reason Sold	Date Sold	

NOTES

_____
_____
_____
_____
_____
_____
_____
_____
_____
_____

DATE	RISK MANAGEMENT
	○ 1-2% of Your Portfolio
	○ Liquidity

TICKER

ENTRY

Execution Price	Where Did You Find The Trade	Purchase Date

WHY

What Indicators Confirmed The Trade

EXIT

Stop Loss Price Level	Profit Target

WHY

Reason Sold	Date Sold

NOTES

_____
_____
_____
_____
_____
_____
_____
_____
_____

DATE	RISK MANAGEMENT
	◯ 1-2% of Your Portfolio
	◯ Liquidity

TICKER

ENTRY

Execution Price	Where Did You Find The Trade	Purchase Date

WHY

What Indicators Confirmed The Trade

EXIT

Stop Loss Price Level	Profit Target

WHY

Reason Sold	Date Sold

NOTES

	DATE	RISK MANAGEMENT
		○ 1-2% of Your Portfolio
		○ Liquidity

TICKER

ENTRY	Execution Price	Where Did You Find The Trade	Purchase Date
WHY	What Indicators Confirmed The Trade		
EXIT	Stop Loss Price Level	Profit Target	
WHY	Reason Sold	Date Sold	

NOTES

	DATE	**RISK MANAGEMENT**
		◯ 1-2% of Your Portfolio
		◯ Liquidity

TICKER

ENTRY

Execution Price	Where Did You Find The Trade	Purchase Date

WHY

What Indicators Confirmed The Trade

EXIT

Stop Loss Price Level	Profit Target

WHY

Reason Sold	Date Sold

NOTES

_____
_____
_____
_____
_____
_____
_____
_____
_____

	DATE	RISK MANAGEMENT
		○ 1-2% of Your Portfolio
		○ Liquidity

TICKER

ENTRY	Execution Price	Where Did You Find The Trade	Purchase Date
WHY	What Indicators Confirmed The Trade		
EXIT	Stop Loss Price Level		Profit Target
WHY	Reason Sold		Date Sold

NOTES

DATE	RISK MANAGEMENT
	◯ 1-2% of Your Portfolio
	◯ Liquidity

TICKER

ENTRY	Execution Price	Where Did You Find The Trade	Purchase Date
WHY	What Indicators Confirmed The Trade		
EXIT	Stop Loss Price Level	Profit Target	
WHY	Reason Sold	Date Sold	

NOTES

	DATE	RISK MANAGEMENT
		○ 1-2% of Your Portfolio
		○ Liquidity

TICKER

ENTRY	Execution Price	Where Did You Find The Trade	Purchase Date
WHY	What Indicators Confirmed The Trade		
EXIT	Stop Loss Price Level	Profit Target	
WHY	Reason Sold	Date Sold	

NOTES

	DATE	**RISK MANAGEMENT**
		○ 1-2% of Your Portfolio
		○ Liquidity

TICKER

ENTRY	Execution Price	Where Did You Find The Trade	Purchase Date
WHY	What Indicators Confirmed The Trade		
EXIT	Stop Loss Price Level	Profit Target	
WHY	Reason Sold	Date Sold	

NOTES

	DATE	**RISK MANAGEMENT**
		⭕ 1-2% of Your Portfolio
		⭕ Liquidity

TICKER

ENTRY	Execution Price	Where Did You Find The Trade	Purchase Date
WHY	What Indicators Confirmed The Trade		
EXIT	Stop Loss Price Level	Profit Target	
WHY	Reason Sold	Date Sold	

NOTES

_____
_____
_____
_____
_____
_____
_____
_____
_____

DATE	RISK MANAGEMENT
	◯ 1-2% of Your Portfolio ◯ Liquidity

TICKER

ENTRY	Execution Price	Where Did You Find The Trade	Purchase Date
WHY	What Indicators Confirmed The Trade		
EXIT	Stop Loss Price Level		Profit Target
WHY	Reason Sold		Date Sold

NOTES

	DATE	**RISK MANAGEMENT**	
		◯ 1-2% of Your Portfolio	
		◯ Liquidity	

TICKER			
ENTRY	Execution Price	Where Did You Find The Trade	Purchase Date
WHY	What Indicators Confirmed The Trade		
EXIT	Stop Loss Price Level	Profit Target	
WHY	Reason Sold	Date Sold	

NOTES

	DATE	**RISK MANAGEMENT**	
		○ 1-2% of Your Portfolio	
		○ Liquidity	

TICKER			
ENTRY	Execution Price	Where Did You Find The Trade	Purchase Date
WHY	What Indicators Confirmed The Trade		
EXIT	Stop Loss Price Level		Profit Target
WHY	Reason Sold		Date Sold

NOTES

_____
_____
_____
_____
_____
_____
_____
_____
_____
_____

DATE	RISK MANAGEMENT
	◯ 1-2% of Your Portfolio ◯ Liquidity

TICKER

ENTRY

Execution Price	Where Did You Find The Trade	Purchase Date

WHY

What Indicators Confirmed The Trade

EXIT

Stop Loss Price Level	Profit Target

WHY

Reason Sold	Date Sold

NOTES

_____
_____
_____
_____
_____
_____
_____
_____
_____

DATE	RISK MANAGEMENT
	○ 1-2% of Your Portfolio
	○ Liquidity

TICKER

ENTRY

Execution Price	Where Did You Find The Trade	Purchase Date

WHY

What Indicators Confirmed The Trade

EXIT

Stop Loss Price Level	Profit Target

WHY

Reason Sold	Date Sold

NOTES

	DATE	**RISK MANAGEMENT**
		◯ 1-2% of Your Portfolio
		◯ Liquidity

TICKER

ENTRY	Execution Price	Where Did You Find The Trade	Purchase Date
WHY	What Indicators Confirmed The Trade		
EXIT	Stop Loss Price Level	Profit Target	
WHY	Reason Sold	Date Sold	

NOTES

_____
_____
_____
_____
_____
_____
_____
_____
_____
_____

	DATE	**RISK MANAGEMENT**
		○ 1-2% of Your Portfolio
		○ Liquidity

TICKER

ENTRY	Execution Price	Where Did You Find The Trade	Purchase Date

WHY	What Indicators Confirmed The Trade	

EXIT	Stop Loss Price Level	Profit Target

WHY	Reason Sold	Date Sold

NOTES

DATE	RISK MANAGEMENT
	◯ 1-2% of Your Portfolio ◯ Liquidity

TICKER

ENTRY	Execution Price	Where Did You Find The Trade	Purchase Date
WHY	What Indicators Confirmed The Trade		
EXIT	Stop Loss Price Level		Profit Target
WHY	Reason Sold		Date Sold

NOTES

DATE	**RISK MANAGEMENT** ◯ 1-2% of Your Portfolio ◯ Liquidity

TICKER

ENTRY	Execution Price	Where Did You Find The Trade	Purchase Date
WHY	What Indicators Confirmed The Trade		
EXIT	Stop Loss Price Level		Profit Target
WHY	Reason Sold		Date Sold

NOTES

DATE	**RISK MANAGEMENT** ◯ 1-2% of Your Portfolio ◯ Liquidity

TICKER

ENTRY	Execution Price	Where Did You Find The Trade	Purchase Date
WHY	What Indicators Confirmed The Trade		
EXIT	Stop Loss Price Level		Profit Target
WHY	Reason Sold		Date Sold

NOTES

_____
_____
_____
_____
_____
_____
_____
_____
_____
_____

	DATE	**RISK MANAGEMENT**
		◯ 1-2% of Your Portfolio
		◯ Liquidity

TICKER

ENTRY	Execution Price	Where Did You Find The Trade	Purchase Date
WHY	What Indicators Confirmed The Trade		
EXIT	Stop Loss Price Level		Profit Target
WHY	Reason Sold		Date Sold

NOTES

_____
_____
_____
_____
_____
_____
_____
_____
_____

	DATE	**RISK MANAGEMENT**	
		◯ 1-2% of Your Portfolio	
		◯ Liquidity	

TICKER

ENTRY	Execution Price	Where Did You Find The Trade	Purchase Date
WHY	What Indicators Confirmed The Trade		
EXIT	Stop Loss Price Level	Profit Target	
WHY	Reason Sold	Date Sold	

NOTES

DATE	RISK MANAGEMENT
	○ 1-2% of Your Portfolio
	○ Liquidity

TICKER

ENTRY

Execution Price	Where Did You Find The Trade	Purchase Date

WHY

What Indicators Confirmed The Trade

EXIT

Stop Loss Price Level	Profit Target

WHY

Reason Sold	Date Sold

NOTES

	DATE	**RISK MANAGEMENT**
		◯ 1-2% of Your Portfolio
		◯ Liquidity

TICKER

ENTRY	Execution Price	Where Did You Find The Trade	Purchase Date
WHY	What Indicators Confirmed The Trade		
EXIT	Stop Loss Price Level		Profit Target
WHY	Reason Sold		Date Sold

NOTES

DATE	RISK MANAGEMENT
	○ 1-2% of Your Portfolio
	○ Liquidity

TICKER

ENTRY	Execution Price	Where Did You Find The Trade	Purchase Date

WHY	What Indicators Confirmed The Trade

EXIT	Stop Loss Price Level	Profit Target

WHY	Reason Sold	Date Sold

NOTES

_____
_____
_____
_____
_____
_____
_____
_____
_____
_____

DATE	RISK MANAGEMENT
	○ 1-2% of Your Portfolio
	○ Liquidity

TICKER

ENTRY

Execution Price	Where Did You Find The Trade	Purchase Date

WHY

What Indicators Confirmed The Trade

EXIT

Stop Loss Price Level	Profit Target

WHY

Reason Sold	Date Sold

NOTES

	DATE	**RISK MANAGEMENT**
		○ 1-2% of Your Portfolio
		○ Liquidity

TICKER

ENTRY	Execution Price	Where Did You Find The Trade	Purchase Date
WHY	What Indicators Confirmed The Trade		
EXIT	Stop Loss Price Level	Profit Target	
WHY	Reason Sold	Date Sold	

NOTES

	DATE	RISK MANAGEMENT
		◯ 1-2% of Your Portfolio
		◯ Liquidity

TICKER

ENTRY	Execution Price	Where Did You Find The Trade	Purchase Date
WHY	What Indicators Confirmed The Trade		
EXIT	Stop Loss Price Level	Profit Target	
WHY	Reason Sold	Date Sold	

NOTES

	DATE	RISK MANAGEMENT
		◯ 1-2% of Your Portfolio
		◯ Liquidity

TICKER

ENTRY	Execution Price	Where Did You Find The Trade	Purchase Date

WHY	What Indicators Confirmed The Trade

EXIT	Stop Loss Price Level	Profit Target

WHY	Reason Sold	Date Sold

NOTES

	DATE	RISK MANAGEMENT
		○ 1-2% of Your Portfolio
		○ Liquidity

TICKER

ENTRY	Execution Price	Where Did You Find The Trade	Purchase Date
WHY	What Indicators Confirmed The Trade		
EXIT	Stop Loss Price Level		Profit Target
WHY	Reason Sold		Date Sold

NOTES

	DATE	**RISK MANAGEMENT**
		◯ 1-2% of Your Portfolio
		◯ Liquidity

TICKER

	Execution Price	Where Did You Find The Trade	Purchase Date
ENTRY			
WHY	What Indicators Confirmed The Trade		
EXIT	Stop Loss Price Level	Profit Target	
WHY	Reason Sold	Date Sold	

NOTES

	DATE	**RISK MANAGEMENT**	
		◯ 1-2% of Your Portfolio	
		◯ Liquidity	

TICKER

ENTRY	Execution Price	Where Did You Find The Trade	Purchase Date
WHY	What Indicators Confirmed The Trade		
EXIT	Stop Loss Price Level	Profit Target	
WHY	Reason Sold	Date Sold	

NOTES

_____
_____
_____
_____
_____
_____
_____
_____
_____

	DATE	RISK MANAGEMENT
		○ 1-2% of Your Portfolio
		○ Liquidity

TICKER

ENTRY	Execution Price	Where Did You Find The Trade	Purchase Date
WHY	What Indicators Confirmed The Trade		
EXIT	Stop Loss Price Level	Profit Target	
WHY	Reason Sold	Date Sold	

NOTES

	DATE	**RISK MANAGEMENT**
		○ 1-2% of Your Portfolio
		○ Liquidity

TICKER

ENTRY	Execution Price	Where Did You Find The Trade	Purchase Date
WHY	What Indicators Confirmed The Trade		
EXIT	Stop Loss Price Level	Profit Target	
WHY	Reason Sold	Date Sold	

NOTES

DATE	RISK MANAGEMENT
	◯ 1-2% of Your Portfolio
	◯ Liquidity

TICKER

ENTRY

Execution Price	Where Did You Find The Trade	Purchase Date

WHY

What Indicators Confirmed The Trade

EXIT

Stop Loss Price Level	Profit Target

WHY

Reason Sold	Date Sold

NOTES

DATE	RISK MANAGEMENT
	○ 1-2% of Your Portfolio
	○ Liquidity

TICKER

ENTRY

Execution Price	Where Did You Find The Trade	Purchase Date

WHY

What Indicators Confirmed The Trade

EXIT

Stop Loss Price Level	Profit Target

WHY

Reason Sold	Date Sold

NOTES

_____
_____
_____
_____
_____
_____
_____
_____
_____

DATE	RISK MANAGEMENT
	◯ 1-2% of Your Portfolio ◯ Liquidity

TICKER

ENTRY

Execution Price	Where Did You Find The Trade	Purchase Date

WHY

What Indicators Confirmed The Trade

EXIT

Stop Loss Price Level	Profit Target

WHY

Reason Sold	Date Sold

NOTES

_____
_____
_____
_____
_____
_____
_____
_____
_____

DATE	**RISK MANAGEMENT**
	⚪ 1-2% of Your Portfolio
	⚪ Liquidity

TICKER

ENTRY	Execution Price	Where Did You Find The Trade	Purchase Date
WHY	What Indicators Confirmed The Trade		
EXIT	Stop Loss Price Level		Profit Target
WHY	Reason Sold		Date Sold

NOTES

	DATE	RISK MANAGEMENT
		○ 1-2% of Your Portfolio
		○ Liquidity

TICKER

ENTRY	Execution Price	Where Did You Find The Trade	Purchase Date
WHY	What Indicators Confirmed The Trade		
EXIT	Stop Loss Price Level		Profit Target
WHY	Reason Sold		Date Sold

NOTES

	DATE	RISK MANAGEMENT
		○ 1-2% of Your Portfolio
		○ Liquidity

TICKER

ENTRY	Execution Price	Where Did You Find The Trade	Purchase Date
WHY	What Indicators Confirmed The Trade		
EXIT	Stop Loss Price Level	Profit Target	
WHY	Reason Sold	Date Sold	

NOTES

	DATE	**RISK MANAGEMENT**
		○ 1-2% of Your Portfolio
		○ Liquidity

TICKER

ENTRY	Execution Price	Where Did You Find The Trade	Purchase Date

WHY	What Indicators Confirmed The Trade		

EXIT	Stop Loss Price Level	Profit Target

WHY	Reason Sold	Date Sold

NOTES

_____
_____
_____
_____
_____
_____
_____
_____
_____
_____

	DATE	**RISK MANAGEMENT**
		◯ 1-2% of Your Portfolio
		◯ Liquidity

TICKER

ENTRY	Execution Price	Where Did You Find The Trade	Purchase Date
WHY	What Indicators Confirmed The Trade		
EXIT	Stop Loss Price Level		Profit Target
WHY	Reason Sold		Date Sold

NOTES

_____
_____
_____
_____
_____
_____
_____
_____
_____
_____

	DATE	**RISK MANAGEMENT**
		◯ 1-2% of Your Portfolio
		◯ Liquidity

TICKER

ENTRY	Execution Price	Where Did You Find The Trade	Purchase Date

WHY	What Indicators Confirmed The Trade

EXIT	Stop Loss Price Level	Profit Target

WHY	Reason Sold	Date Sold

NOTES

DATE	RISK MANAGEMENT
	◯ 1-2% of Your Portfolio
	◯ Liquidity

TICKER

ENTRY	Execution Price	Where Did You Find The Trade	Purchase Date
WHY	What Indicators Confirmed The Trade		
EXIT	Stop Loss Price Level	Profit Target	
WHY	Reason Sold	Date Sold	

NOTES

_____
_____
_____
_____
_____
_____
_____
_____
_____

	DATE	**RISK MANAGEMENT**
		◯ 1-2% of Your Portfolio
		◯ Liquidity

TICKER

ENTRY	Execution Price	Where Did You Find The Trade	Purchase Date
WHY	What Indicators Confirmed The Trade		
EXIT	Stop Loss Price Level		Profit Target
WHY	Reason Sold		Date Sold

NOTES

	DATE	RISK MANAGEMENT
		○ 1-2% of Your Portfolio
		○ Liquidity

TICKER

ENTRY	Execution Price	Where Did You Find The Trade	Purchase Date
WHY	What Indicators Confirmed The Trade		
EXIT	Stop Loss Price Level		Profit Target
WHY	Reason Sold		Date Sold

NOTES

	DATE	RISK MANAGEMENT	
		◯ 1-2% of Your Portfolio ◯ Liquidity	

TICKER			
ENTRY	Execution Price	Where Did You Find The Trade	Purchase Date
WHY	What Indicators Confirmed The Trade		
EXIT	Stop Loss Price Level		Profit Target
WHY	Reason Sold		Date Sold

NOTES

	DATE	**RISK MANAGEMENT**
		◯ 1-2% of Your Portfolio
		◯ Liquidity

TICKER

ENTRY	Execution Price	Where Did You Find The Trade	Purchase Date
WHY	What Indicators Confirmed The Trade		
EXIT	Stop Loss Price Level	Profit Target	
WHY	Reason Sold	Date Sold	

NOTES

	DATE	RISK MANAGEMENT
		◯ 1-2% of Your Portfolio
		◯ Liquidity

TICKER

ENTRY

Execution Price	Where Did You Find The Trade	Purchase Date

WHY

What Indicators Confirmed The Trade

EXIT

Stop Loss Price Level	Profit Target

WHY

Reason Sold	Date Sold

NOTES

DATE	RISK MANAGEMENT
	○ 1-2% of Your Portfolio
	○ Liquidity

TICKER

ENTRY	Execution Price	Where Did You Find The Trade	Purchase Date

WHY	What Indicators Confirmed The Trade

EXIT	Stop Loss Price Level	Profit Target

WHY	Reason Sold	Date Sold

NOTES

_____

_____

_____

_____

_____

_____

_____

_____

	DATE	**RISK MANAGEMENT**
		◯ 1-2% of Your Portfolio
		◯ Liquidity

TICKER

ENTRY	Execution Price	Where Did You Find The Trade	Purchase Date

WHY	What Indicators Confirmed The Trade

EXIT	Stop Loss Price Level	Profit Target

WHY	Reason Sold	Date Sold

NOTES

_____
_____
_____
_____
_____
_____
_____
_____
_____
_____

DATE	RISK MANAGEMENT
	○ 1-2% of Your Portfolio
	○ Liquidity

TICKER

ENTRY	Execution Price	Where Did You Find The Trade	Purchase Date

WHY	What Indicators Confirmed The Trade

EXIT	Stop Loss Price Level	Profit Target

WHY	Reason Sold	Date Sold

NOTES

_____
_____
_____
_____
_____
_____
_____
_____
_____

DATE	RISK MANAGEMENT
	○ 1-2% of Your Portfolio
	○ Liquidity

TICKER

ENTRY

Execution Price	Where Did You Find The Trade	Purchase Date

WHY

What Indicators Confirmed The Trade

EXIT

Stop Loss Price Level	Profit Target

WHY

Reason Sold	Date Sold

NOTES

	DATE	RISK MANAGEMENT
		◯ 1-2% of Your Portfolio
		◯ Liquidity

TICKER

ENTRY	Execution Price	Where Did You Find The Trade	Purchase Date
WHY	What Indicators Confirmed The Trade		
EXIT	Stop Loss Price Level	Profit Target	
WHY	Reason Sold	Date Sold	

NOTES

DATE	RISK MANAGEMENT
	○ 1-2% of Your Portfolio
	○ Liquidity

TICKER

ENTRY

Execution Price	Where Did You Find The Trade	Purchase Date

WHY

What Indicators Confirmed The Trade

EXIT

Stop Loss Price Level	Profit Target

WHY

Reason Sold	Date Sold

NOTES

DATE	RISK MANAGEMENT
	◯ 1-2% of Your Portfolio
	◯ Liquidity

TICKER

ENTRY	Execution Price	Where Did You Find The Trade	Purchase Date

WHY	What Indicators Confirmed The Trade

	Stop Loss Price Level	Profit Target
EXIT		

	Reason Sold	Date Sold
WHY		

NOTES

	DATE	**RISK MANAGEMENT**
		◯ 1-2% of Your Portfolio
		◯ Liquidity

TICKER			
ENTRY	Execution Price	Where Did You Find The Trade	Purchase Date
WHY	What Indicators Confirmed The Trade		
EXIT	Stop Loss Price Level		Profit Target
WHY	Reason Sold		Date Sold

NOTES

_____
_____
_____
_____
_____
_____
_____
_____
_____

DATE	**RISK MANAGEMENT** ○ 1-2% of Your Portfolio ○ Liquidity

TICKER			
ENTRY	Execution Price	Where Did You Find The Trade	Purchase Date
WHY	What Indicators Confirmed The Trade		
EXIT	Stop Loss Price Level		Profit Target
WHY	Reason Sold		Date Sold

NOTES

_____
_____
_____
_____
_____
_____
_____
_____
_____

DATE	**RISK MANAGEMENT** ◯ 1-2% of Your Portfolio ◯ Liquidity

TICKER

ENTRY	Execution Price	Where Did You Find The Trade	Purchase Date

WHY	What Indicators Confirmed The Trade

EXIT	Stop Loss Price Level	Profit Target

WHY	Reason Sold	Date Sold

NOTES

DATE	RISK MANAGEMENT
	○ 1-2% of Your Portfolio
	○ Liquidity

TICKER

ENTRY

Execution Price	Where Did You Find The Trade	Purchase Date

WHY

What Indicators Confirmed The Trade

EXIT

Stop Loss Price Level	Profit Target

WHY

Reason Sold	Date Sold

NOTES

DATE	RISK MANAGEMENT
	◯ 1-2% of Your Portfolio
	◯ Liquidity

TICKER

ENTRY	Execution Price	Where Did You Find The Trade	Purchase Date
WHY	What Indicators Confirmed The Trade		
EXIT	Stop Loss Price Level		Profit Target
WHY	Reason Sold		Date Sold

NOTES

_____
_____
_____
_____
_____
_____
_____
_____
_____

DATE	**RISK MANAGEMENT**
	○ 1-2% of Your Portfolio
	○ Liquidity

TICKER

ENTRY

Execution Price	Where Did You Find The Trade	Purchase Date

WHY

What Indicators Confirmed The Trade

EXIT

Stop Loss Price Level	Profit Target

WHY

Reason Sold	Date Sold

NOTES

_____
_____
_____
_____
_____
_____
_____
_____
_____

	DATE	**RISK MANAGEMENT**
		◯ 1-2% of Your Portfolio
		◯ Liquidity

TICKER

ENTRY	Execution Price	Where Did You Find The Trade	Purchase Date
WHY	What Indicators Confirmed The Trade		
EXIT	Stop Loss Price Level		Profit Target
WHY	Reason Sold		Date Sold

NOTES

DATE	RISK MANAGEMENT
	○ 1-2% of Your Portfolio
	○ Liquidity

TICKER

ENTRY

Execution Price	Where Did You Find The Trade	Purchase Date

WHY

What Indicators Confirmed The Trade

EXIT

Stop Loss Price Level	Profit Target

WHY

Reason Sold	Date Sold

NOTES

	DATE	**RISK MANAGEMENT**
		○ 1-2% of Your Portfolio
		○ Liquidity

TICKER

ENTRY	Execution Price	Where Did You Find The Trade	Purchase Date

WHY	What Indicators Confirmed The Trade	

EXIT	Stop Loss Price Level	Profit Target

WHY	Reason Sold	Date Sold

NOTES

DATE	RISK MANAGEMENT
	◯ 1-2% of Your Portfolio ◯ Liquidity

TICKER

ENTRY	Execution Price	Where Did You Find The Trade	Purchase Date
WHY	What Indicators Confirmed The Trade		
EXIT	Stop Loss Price Level	Profit Target	
WHY	Reason Sold	Date Sold	

NOTES

_____
_____
_____
_____
_____
_____
_____
_____
_____
_____

	DATE	RISK MANAGEMENT
		○ 1-2% of Your Portfolio
		○ Liquidity

TICKER

ENTRY	Execution Price	Where Did You Find The Trade	Purchase Date
WHY	What Indicators Confirmed The Trade		
EXIT	Stop Loss Price Level	Profit Target	
WHY	Reason Sold	Date Sold	

NOTES

DATE	RISK MANAGEMENT
	◯ 1-2% of Your Portfolio
	◯ Liquidity

TICKER

ENTRY	Execution Price	Where Did You Find The Trade	Purchase Date
WHY	What Indicators Confirmed The Trade		
EXIT	Stop Loss Price Level		Profit Target
WHY	Reason Sold		Date Sold

NOTES

DATE	RISK MANAGEMENT
	◯ 1-2% of Your Portfolio ◯ Liquidity

TICKER

ENTRY

Execution Price	Where Did You Find The Trade	Purchase Date

WHY

What Indicators Confirmed The Trade

EXIT

Stop Loss Price Level	Profit Target

WHY

Reason Sold	Date Sold

NOTES

	DATE	**RISK MANAGEMENT**
		◯ 1-2% of Your Portfolio
		◯ Liquidity

TICKER

ENTRY	Execution Price	Where Did You Find The Trade	Purchase Date
WHY	What Indicators Confirmed The Trade		
EXIT	Stop Loss Price Level		Profit Target
WHY	Reason Sold		Date Sold

NOTES

_____

_____

_____

_____

_____

_____

_____

_____

_____

	DATE	**RISK MANAGEMENT**
		◯ 1-2% of Your Portfolio
		◯ Liquidity

TICKER

ENTRY	Execution Price	Where Did You Find The Trade	Purchase Date
WHY	What Indicators Confirmed The Trade		
EXIT	Stop Loss Price Level		Profit Target
WHY	Reason Sold		Date Sold

NOTES

_____
_____
_____
_____
_____
_____
_____
_____
_____
_____

	DATE	**RISK MANAGEMENT**
		○ 1-2% of Your Portfolio
		○ Liquidity

TICKER

ENTRY	Execution Price	Where Did You Find The Trade	Purchase Date
WHY	What Indicators Confirmed The Trade		
EXIT	Stop Loss Price Level		Profit Target
WHY	Reason Sold		Date Sold

NOTES

DATE	RISK MANAGEMENT
	◯ 1-2% of Your Portfolio
	◯ Liquidity

TICKER

ENTRY

Execution Price	Where Did You Find The Trade	Purchase Date

WHY

What Indicators Confirmed The Trade

EXIT

Stop Loss Price Level	Profit Target

WHY

Reason Sold	Date Sold

NOTES

	DATE	**RISK MANAGEMENT**
		○ 1-2% of Your Portfolio
		○ Liquidity

TICKER

ENTRY

Execution Price	Where Did You Find The Trade	Purchase Date

WHY

What Indicators Confirmed The Trade

EXIT

Stop Loss Price Level	Profit Target

WHY

Reason Sold	Date Sold

NOTES

DATE	RISK MANAGEMENT
	○ 1-2% of Your Portfolio
	○ Liquidity

TICKER

ENTRY	Execution Price	Where Did You Find The Trade	Purchase Date

WHY	What Indicators Confirmed The Trade

EXIT	Stop Loss Price Level	Profit Target

WHY	Reason Sold	Date Sold

NOTES

	DATE	RISK MANAGEMENT
		○ 1-2% of Your Portfolio
		○ Liquidity

TICKER

	Execution Price	Where Did You Find The Trade	Purchase Date
ENTRY			

	What Indicators Confirmed The Trade
WHY	

	Stop Loss Price Level	Profit Target
EXIT		

	Reason Sold	Date Sold
WHY		

NOTES

	DATE	**RISK MANAGEMENT**
		◯ 1-2% of Your Portfolio
		◯ Liquidity

TICKER

ENTRY	Execution Price	Where Did You Find The Trade	Purchase Date

WHY	What Indicators Confirmed The Trade

EXIT	Stop Loss Price Level	Profit Target

WHY	Reason Sold	Date Sold

NOTES

DATE	RISK MANAGEMENT
	○ 1-2% of Your Portfolio ○ Liquidity

TICKER

ENTRY	Execution Price	Where Did You Find The Trade	Purchase Date
WHY	What Indicators Confirmed The Trade		
EXIT	Stop Loss Price Level		Profit Target
WHY	Reason Sold		Date Sold

NOTES

	DATE	**RISK MANAGEMENT**
		◯ 1-2% of Your Portfolio
		◯ Liquidity

TICKER

ENTRY	Execution Price	Where Did You Find The Trade	Purchase Date

WHY	What Indicators Confirmed The Trade

EXIT	Stop Loss Price Level	Profit Target

WHY	Reason Sold	Date Sold

NOTES

DATE	**RISK MANAGEMENT**
	◯ 1-2% of Your Portfolio
	◯ Liquidity

TICKER

ENTRY

Execution Price	Where Did You Find The Trade	Purchase Date

WHY

What Indicators Confirmed The Trade

EXIT

Stop Loss Price Level	Profit Target

WHY

Reason Sold	Date Sold

NOTES

_____
_____
_____
_____
_____
_____
_____
_____
_____

	DATE	RISK MANAGEMENT
		○ 1-2% of Your Portfolio
		○ Liquidity

TICKER

ENTRY

Execution Price	Where Did You Find The Trade	Purchase Date

WHY

What Indicators Confirmed The Trade

EXIT

Stop Loss Price Level	Profit Target

WHY

Reason Sold	Date Sold

NOTES

DATE	**RISK MANAGEMENT**
	◯ 1-2% of Your Portfolio
	◯ Liquidity

TICKER

ENTRY	Execution Price	Where Did You Find The Trade	Purchase Date
WHY	What Indicators Confirmed The Trade		
EXIT	Stop Loss Price Level		Profit Target
WHY	Reason Sold		Date Sold

NOTES

DATE	RISK MANAGEMENT
	◯ 1-2% of Your Portfolio
	◯ Liquidity

TICKER

ENTRY	Execution Price	Where Did You Find The Trade	Purchase Date

WHY	What Indicators Confirmed The Trade

EXIT	Stop Loss Price Level	Profit Target

WHY	Reason Sold	Date Sold

NOTES

DATE	RISK MANAGEMENT
	◯ 1-2% of Your Portfolio
	◯ Liquidity

TICKER

ENTRY

Execution Price	Where Did You Find The Trade	Purchase Date

WHY

What Indicators Confirmed The Trade

EXIT

Stop Loss Price Level	Profit Target

WHY

Reason Sold	Date Sold

NOTES

	DATE	RISK MANAGEMENT
		⚪ 1-2% of Your Portfolio ⚪ Liquidity

TICKER			
ENTRY	Execution Price	Where Did You Find The Trade	Purchase Date
WHY	What Indicators Confirmed The Trade		
EXIT	Stop Loss Price Level		Profit Target
WHY	Reason Sold		Date Sold

NOTES

	DATE	**RISK MANAGEMENT**
		○ 1-2% of Your Portfolio
		○ Liquidity

TICKER

ENTRY	Execution Price	Where Did You Find The Trade	Purchase Date
WHY	What Indicators Confirmed The Trade		
EXIT	Stop Loss Price Level		Profit Target
WHY	Reason Sold		Date Sold

NOTES

_____
_____
_____
_____
_____
_____
_____
_____
_____

DATE	RISK MANAGEMENT
	○ 1-2% of Your Portfolio
	○ Liquidity

TICKER

ENTRY

Execution Price	Where Did You Find The Trade	Purchase Date

WHY

What Indicators Confirmed The Trade

EXIT

Stop Loss Price Level	Profit Target

WHY

Reason Sold	Date Sold

NOTES

	DATE	RISK MANAGEMENT
		○ 1-2% of Your Portfolio
		○ Liquidity

TICKER

ENTRY	Execution Price	Where Did You Find The Trade	Purchase Date

WHY	What Indicators Confirmed The Trade

EXIT	Stop Loss Price Level	Profit Target

WHY	Reason Sold	Date Sold

NOTES

	DATE		**RISK MANAGEMENT** ◯ 1-2% of Your Portfolio ◯ Liquidity	
TICKER				
ENTRY	Execution Price	Where Did You Find The Trade		Purchase Date
WHY	What Indicators Confirmed The Trade			
EXIT	Stop Loss Price Level		Profit Target	
WHY	Reason Sold		Date Sold	

NOTES

	DATE	**RISK MANAGEMENT**
		◯ 1-2% of Your Portfolio
		◯ Liquidity

TICKER			
ENTRY	Execution Price	Where Did You Find The Trade	Purchase Date
WHY	What Indicators Confirmed The Trade		
EXIT	Stop Loss Price Level		Profit Target
WHY	Reason Sold		Date Sold

NOTES

_____
_____
_____
_____
_____
_____
_____
_____
_____

	DATE	**RISK MANAGEMENT**	
		◯ 1-2% of Your Portfolio	
		◯ Liquidity	

TICKER			
ENTRY	Execution Price	Where Did You Find The Trade	Purchase Date
WHY	What Indicators Confirmed The Trade		
EXIT	Stop Loss Price Level	Profit Target	
WHY	Reason Sold	Date Sold	

NOTES

	DATE	**RISK MANAGEMENT**
		◯ 1-2% of Your Portfolio
		◯ Liquidity

TICKER

ENTRY	Execution Price	Where Did You Find The Trade	Purchase Date
WHY	What Indicators Confirmed The Trade		
EXIT	Stop Loss Price Level		Profit Target
WHY	Reason Sold		Date Sold

NOTES

_____
_____
_____
_____
_____
_____
_____
_____
_____

DATE	RISK MANAGEMENT
	◯ 1-2% of Your Portfolio
	◯ Liquidity

TICKER

ENTRY	Execution Price	Where Did You Find The Trade	Purchase Date

WHY	What Indicators Confirmed The Trade

EXIT	Stop Loss Price Level	Profit Target

WHY	Reason Sold	Date Sold

NOTES

	DATE	**RISK MANAGEMENT**
		○ 1-2% of Your Portfolio
		○ Liquidity

TICKER			
ENTRY	Execution Price	Where Did You Find The Trade	Purchase Date
WHY	What Indicators Confirmed The Trade		
EXIT	Stop Loss Price Level		Profit Target
WHY	Reason Sold		Date Sold

NOTES

_____
_____
_____
_____
_____
_____
_____
_____
_____

	DATE	**RISK MANAGEMENT**
		◯ 1-2% of Your Portfolio
		◯ Liquidity

TICKER			
ENTRY	Execution Price	Where Did You Find The Trade	Purchase Date
WHY	What Indicators Confirmed The Trade		
EXIT	Stop Loss Price Level		Profit Target
WHY	Reason Sold		Date Sold

NOTES

	DATE	RISK MANAGEMENT
		○ 1-2% of Your Portfolio
		○ Liquidity

TICKER

ENTRY	Execution Price	Where Did You Find The Trade	Purchase Date
WHY	What Indicators Confirmed The Trade		
EXIT	Stop Loss Price Level		Profit Target
WHY	Reason Sold		Date Sold

NOTES

	DATE	**RISK MANAGEMENT**	
		◯ 1-2% of Your Portfolio	
		◯ Liquidity	

TICKER			
ENTRY	Execution Price	Where Did You Find The Trade	Purchase Date
WHY	What Indicators Confirmed The Trade		
EXIT	Stop Loss Price Level	Profit Target	
WHY	Reason Sold	Date Sold	

NOTES

DATE	RISK MANAGEMENT
	○ 1-2% of Your Portfolio
	○ Liquidity

TICKER

ENTRY

Execution Price	Where Did You Find The Trade	Purchase Date

WHY

What Indicators Confirmed The Trade

EXIT

Stop Loss Price Level	Profit Target

WHY

Reason Sold	Date Sold

NOTES

	DATE	**RISK MANAGEMENT**
		◯ 1-2% of Your Portfolio
		◯ Liquidity

TICKER

ENTRY	Execution Price	Where Did You Find The Trade	Purchase Date
WHY	What Indicators Confirmed The Trade		
EXIT	Stop Loss Price Level		Profit Target
WHY	Reason Sold		Date Sold

NOTES

DATE	RISK MANAGEMENT
	○ 1-2% of Your Portfolio
	○ Liquidity

TICKER

ENTRY	Execution Price	Where Did You Find The Trade	Purchase Date

WHY	What Indicators Confirmed The Trade

EXIT	Stop Loss Price Level	Profit Target

WHY	Reason Sold	Date Sold

NOTES

	DATE	**RISK MANAGEMENT**	
		◯ 1-2% of Your Portfolio	
		◯ Liquidity	

TICKER

ENTRY	Execution Price	Where Did You Find The Trade	Purchase Date

WHY	What Indicators Confirmed The Trade

EXIT	Stop Loss Price Level	Profit Target

WHY	Reason Sold	Date Sold

NOTES

	DATE	**RISK MANAGEMENT**
		◯ 1-2% of Your Portfolio
		◯ Liquidity

TICKER

ENTRY	Execution Price	Where Did You Find The Trade	Purchase Date
WHY	What Indicators Confirmed The Trade		
EXIT	Stop Loss Price Level		Profit Target
WHY	Reason Sold		Date Sold

NOTES

	DATE	**RISK MANAGEMENT**	
		◯ 1-2% of Your Portfolio	
		◯ Liquidity	

TICKER			
ENTRY	Execution Price	Where Did You Find The Trade	Purchase Date
WHY	What Indicators Confirmed The Trade		
EXIT	Stop Loss Price Level		Profit Target
WHY	Reason Sold		Date Sold

NOTES

	DATE	**RISK MANAGEMENT**
		◯ 1-2% of Your Portfolio
		◯ Liquidity

TICKER

ENTRY	Execution Price	Where Did You Find The Trade	Purchase Date
WHY	What Indicators Confirmed The Trade		
EXIT	Stop Loss Price Level		Profit Target
WHY	Reason Sold		Date Sold

NOTES

_____
_____
_____
_____
_____
_____
_____
_____
_____

	DATE	**RISK MANAGEMENT**
		◯ 1-2% of Your Portfolio
		◯ Liquidity

TICKER

ENTRY

Execution Price	Where Did You Find The Trade	Purchase Date

WHY

What Indicators Confirmed The Trade

EXIT

Stop Loss Price Level	Profit Target

WHY

Reason Sold	Date Sold

NOTES

	DATE	**RISK MANAGEMENT**
		◯ 1-2% of Your Portfolio
		◯ Liquidity

TICKER

ENTRY	Execution Price	Where Did You Find The Trade	Purchase Date
WHY	What Indicators Confirmed The Trade		
EXIT	Stop Loss Price Level		Profit Target
WHY	Reason Sold		Date Sold

NOTES

	DATE	RISK MANAGEMENT
		○ 1-2% of Your Portfolio
		○ Liquidity

TICKER

ENTRY	Execution Price	Where Did You Find The Trade	Purchase Date
WHY	What Indicators Confirmed The Trade		
EXIT	Stop Loss Price Level	Profit Target	
WHY	Reason Sold	Date Sold	

NOTES

DATE	RISK MANAGEMENT
	◯ 1-2% of Your Portfolio ◯ Liquidity

TICKER

ENTRY	Execution Price	Where Did You Find The Trade	Purchase Date
WHY	What Indicators Confirmed The Trade		
EXIT	Stop Loss Price Level	Profit Target	
WHY	Reason Sold	Date Sold	

NOTES

DATE	RISK MANAGEMENT
	◯ 1-2% of Your Portfolio
	◯ Liquidity

TICKER

ENTRY	Execution Price	Where Did You Find The Trade	Purchase Date

WHY	What Indicators Confirmed The Trade

EXIT	Stop Loss Price Level	Profit Target

WHY	Reason Sold	Date Sold

NOTES

	DATE	RISK MANAGEMENT
		◯ 1-2% of Your Portfolio
		◯ Liquidity

TICKER

ENTRY	Execution Price	Where Did You Find The Trade	Purchase Date
WHY	What Indicators Confirmed The Trade		
EXIT	Stop Loss Price Level	Profit Target	
WHY	Reason Sold	Date Sold	

NOTES

DATE	**RISK MANAGEMENT**
	○ 1-2% of Your Portfolio
	○ Liquidity

TICKER			
ENTRY	Execution Price	Where Did You Find The Trade	Purchase Date
WHY	What Indicators Confirmed The Trade		
EXIT	Stop Loss Price Level	Profit Target	
WHY	Reason Sold	Date Sold	

NOTES

	DATE	RISK MANAGEMENT
		○ 1-2% of Your Portfolio
		○ Liquidity

TICKER

ENTRY	Execution Price	Where Did You Find The Trade	Purchase Date
WHY	What Indicators Confirmed The Trade		
EXIT	Stop Loss Price Level		Profit Target
WHY	Reason Sold		Date Sold

NOTES

	DATE	**RISK MANAGEMENT**
		◯ 1-2% of Your Portfolio
		◯ Liquidity

TICKER

ENTRY	Execution Price	Where Did You Find The Trade	Purchase Date

WHY	What Indicators Confirmed The Trade

EXIT	Stop Loss Price Level	Profit Target

WHY	Reason Sold	Date Sold

NOTES

	DATE	**RISK MANAGEMENT**
		◯ 1-2% of Your Portfolio
		◯ Liquidity

TICKER

ENTRY	Execution Price	Where Did You Find The Trade	Purchase Date

WHY	What Indicators Confirmed The Trade

EXIT	Stop Loss Price Level	Profit Target

WHY	Reason Sold	Date Sold

NOTES

_____
_____
_____
_____
_____
_____
_____
_____
_____

	DATE		**RISK MANAGEMENT**	
			◯ 1-2% of Your Portfolio	
			◯ Liquidity	
TICKER				
ENTRY	Execution Price	Where Did You Find The Trade		Purchase Date
WHY	What Indicators Confirmed The Trade			
EXIT	Stop Loss Price Level		Profit Target	
WHY	Reason Sold		Date Sold	

NOTES

	DATE	**RISK MANAGEMENT**
		◯ 1-2% of Your Portfolio
		◯ Liquidity

TICKER			
ENTRY	Execution Price	Where Did You Find The Trade	Purchase Date
WHY	What Indicators Confirmed The Trade		
EXIT	Stop Loss Price Level		Profit Target
WHY	Reason Sold		Date Sold

NOTES

_____
_____
_____
_____
_____
_____
_____
_____
_____
_____

DATE	RISK MANAGEMENT
	◯ 1-2% of Your Portfolio ◯ Liquidity

TICKER

ENTRY

Execution Price	Where Did You Find The Trade	Purchase Date

WHY

What Indicators Confirmed The Trade

EXIT

Stop Loss Price Level	Profit Target

WHY

Reason Sold	Date Sold

NOTES

	DATE	**RISK MANAGEMENT**
		◯ 1-2% of Your Portfolio
		◯ Liquidity

TICKER			
ENTRY	Execution Price	Where Did You Find The Trade	Purchase Date
WHY	What Indicators Confirmed The Trade		
EXIT	Stop Loss Price Level		Profit Target
WHY	Reason Sold		Date Sold

NOTES

	DATE	**RISK MANAGEMENT**
		◯ 1-2% of Your Portfolio
		◯ Liquidity

TICKER

ENTRY	Execution Price	Where Did You Find The Trade	Purchase Date
WHY	What Indicators Confirmed The Trade		
EXIT	Stop Loss Price Level	Profit Target	
WHY	Reason Sold	Date Sold	

NOTES

	DATE	**RISK MANAGEMENT**
		◯ 1-2% of Your Portfolio
		◯ Liquidity

TICKER

ENTRY	Execution Price	Where Did You Find The Trade	Purchase Date

WHY	What Indicators Confirmed The Trade

	Stop Loss Price Level	Profit Target
EXIT		

	Reason Sold	Date Sold
WHY		

NOTES

_____
_____
_____
_____
_____
_____
_____
_____
_____

	DATE	**RISK MANAGEMENT**
		◯ 1-2% of Your Portfolio
		◯ Liquidity

TICKER

ENTRY	Execution Price	Where Did You Find The Trade	Purchase Date
WHY	What Indicators Confirmed The Trade		
EXIT	Stop Loss Price Level	Profit Target	
WHY	Reason Sold	Date Sold	

NOTES

_____
_____
_____
_____
_____
_____
_____
_____
_____
_____

	DATE	**RISK MANAGEMENT**
		◯ 1-2% of Your Portfolio
		◯ Liquidity

TICKER

ENTRY	Execution Price	Where Did You Find The Trade	Purchase Date
WHY	What Indicators Confirmed The Trade		
EXIT	Stop Loss Price Level	Profit Target	
WHY	Reason Sold	Date Sold	

NOTES

	DATE	RISK MANAGEMENT
		◯ 1-2% of Your Portfolio
		◯ Liquidity

TICKER

ENTRY	Execution Price	Where Did You Find The Trade	Purchase Date
WHY	What Indicators Confirmed The Trade		
EXIT	Stop Loss Price Level	Profit Target	
WHY	Reason Sold	Date Sold	

NOTES

DATE	RISK MANAGEMENT
	○ 1-2% of Your Portfolio
	○ Liquidity

TICKER

ENTRY

Execution Price	Where Did You Find The Trade	Purchase Date

WHY

What Indicators Confirmed The Trade

EXIT

Stop Loss Price Level	Profit Target

WHY

Reason Sold	Date Sold

NOTES

	DATE	**RISK MANAGEMENT** ◯ 1-2% of Your Portfolio ◯ Liquidity	
TICKER			
ENTRY	Execution Price	Where Did You Find The Trade	Purchase Date
WHY	What Indicators Confirmed The Trade		
EXIT	Stop Loss Price Level	Profit Target	
WHY	Reason Sold	Date Sold	

NOTES

	DATE	**RISK MANAGEMENT**
		◯ 1-2% of Your Portfolio
		◯ Liquidity

TICKER

ENTRY

Execution Price	Where Did You Find The Trade	Purchase Date

WHY

What Indicators Confirmed The Trade

EXIT

Stop Loss Price Level	Profit Target

WHY

Reason Sold	Date Sold

NOTES

_____
_____
_____
_____
_____
_____
_____
_____
_____

DATE	RISK MANAGEMENT
	◯ 1-2% of Your Portfolio ◯ Liquidity

TICKER

ENTRY

Execution Price	Where Did You Find The Trade	Purchase Date

WHY

What Indicators Confirmed The Trade

EXIT

Stop Loss Price Level	Profit Target

WHY

Reason Sold	Date Sold

NOTES

DATE	RISK MANAGEMENT
	◯ 1-2% of Your Portfolio
	◯ Liquidity

TICKER

ENTRY	Execution Price	Where Did You Find The Trade	Purchase Date

WHY	What Indicators Confirmed The Trade

EXIT	Stop Loss Price Level	Profit Target

WHY	Reason Sold	Date Sold

NOTES

	DATE	**RISK MANAGEMENT**
		◯ 1-2% of Your Portfolio
		◯ Liquidity

TICKER

ENTRY	Execution Price	Where Did You Find The Trade	Purchase Date
WHY	What Indicators Confirmed The Trade		
EXIT	Stop Loss Price Level		Profit Target
WHY	Reason Sold		Date Sold

NOTES

	DATE	**RISK MANAGEMENT**
		◯ 1-2% of Your Portfolio
		◯ Liquidity

TICKER			
ENTRY	Execution Price	Where Did You Find The Trade	Purchase Date
WHY	What Indicators Confirmed The Trade		
EXIT	Stop Loss Price Level		Profit Target
WHY	Reason Sold		Date Sold

NOTES

	DATE	**RISK MANAGEMENT**
		◯ 1-2% of Your Portfolio
		◯ Liquidity

TICKER

ENTRY	Execution Price	Where Did You Find The Trade	Purchase Date
WHY	What Indicators Confirmed The Trade		
EXIT	Stop Loss Price Level		Profit Target
WHY	Reason Sold		Date Sold

NOTES

	DATE	**RISK MANAGEMENT**
		○ 1-2% of Your Portfolio
		○ Liquidity

TICKER			
ENTRY	Execution Price	Where Did You Find The Trade	Purchase Date
WHY	What Indicators Confirmed The Trade		
EXIT	Stop Loss Price Level	Profit Target	
WHY	Reason Sold	Date Sold	

NOTES

_____
_____
_____
_____
_____
_____
_____
_____
_____

	DATE	RISK MANAGEMENT
		○ 1-2% of Your Portfolio
		○ Liquidity

TICKER

ENTRY	Execution Price	Where Did You Find The Trade	Purchase Date

WHY	What Indicators Confirmed The Trade

EXIT	Stop Loss Price Level	Profit Target

WHY	Reason Sold	Date Sold

NOTES

	DATE	**RISK MANAGEMENT**
		◯ 1-2% of Your Portfolio
		◯ Liquidity

TICKER

ENTRY	Execution Price	Where Did You Find The Trade	Purchase Date

WHY	What Indicators Confirmed The Trade

EXIT	Stop Loss Price Level	Profit Target

WHY	Reason Sold	Date Sold

NOTES

_____
_____
_____
_____
_____
_____
_____
_____
_____

DATE	RISK MANAGEMENT
	○ 1-2% of Your Portfolio
	○ Liquidity

TICKER

ENTRY	Execution Price	Where Did You Find The Trade	Purchase Date

WHY	What Indicators Confirmed The Trade

EXIT	Stop Loss Price Level	Profit Target

WHY	Reason Sold	Date Sold

NOTES

DATE	RISK MANAGEMENT
	◯ 1-2% of Your Portfolio ◯ Liquidity

TICKER

ENTRY

Execution Price	Where Did You Find The Trade	Purchase Date

WHY

What Indicators Confirmed The Trade

EXIT

Stop Loss Price Level	Profit Target

WHY

Reason Sold	Date Sold

NOTES

DATE	RISK MANAGEMENT
	◯ 1-2% of Your Portfolio
	◯ Liquidity

TICKER

ENTRY

Execution Price	Where Did You Find The Trade	Purchase Date

WHY

What Indicators Confirmed The Trade

EXIT

Stop Loss Price Level	Profit Target

WHY

Reason Sold	Date Sold

NOTES

	DATE	**RISK MANAGEMENT**
		○ 1-2% of Your Portfolio
		○ Liquidity

TICKER

ENTRY	Execution Price	Where Did You Find The Trade	Purchase Date

WHY	What Indicators Confirmed The Trade

EXIT	Stop Loss Price Level	Profit Target

WHY	Reason Sold	Date Sold

NOTES

DATE	RISK MANAGEMENT
	◯ 1-2% of Your Portfolio
	◯ Liquidity

TICKER

ENTRY	Execution Price	Where Did You Find The Trade	Purchase Date
WHY	What Indicators Confirmed The Trade		
EXIT	Stop Loss Price Level	Profit Target	
WHY	Reason Sold	Date Sold	

NOTES

_____
_____
_____
_____
_____
_____
_____
_____
_____
_____

DATE	RISK MANAGEMENT
	○ 1-2% of Your Portfolio
	○ Liquidity

TICKER

ENTRY	Execution Price	Where Did You Find The Trade	Purchase Date
WHY	What Indicators Confirmed The Trade		
EXIT	Stop Loss Price Level	Profit Target	
WHY	Reason Sold	Date Sold	

NOTES

DATE	RISK MANAGEMENT
	◯ 1-2% of Your Portfolio
	◯ Liquidity

TICKER

ENTRY	Execution Price	Where Did You Find The Trade	Purchase Date

WHY	What Indicators Confirmed The Trade

EXIT	Stop Loss Price Level	Profit Target

WHY	Reason Sold	Date Sold

NOTES

DATE	RISK MANAGEMENT
	○ 1-2% of Your Portfolio
	○ Liquidity

TICKER

ENTRY

Execution Price	Where Did You Find The Trade	Purchase Date

WHY

What Indicators Confirmed The Trade

EXIT

Stop Loss Price Level	Profit Target

WHY

Reason Sold	Date Sold

NOTES

_____
_____
_____
_____
_____
_____
_____
_____
_____

	DATE	**RISK MANAGEMENT**
		◯ 1-2% of Your Portfolio
		◯ Liquidity

TICKER

	Execution Price	Where Did You Find The Trade	Purchase Date
ENTRY			

	What Indicators Confirmed The Trade
WHY	

	Stop Loss Price Level	Profit Target
EXIT		

	Reason Sold	Date Sold
WHY		

NOTES

	DATE	**RISK MANAGEMENT**
		◯ 1-2% of Your Portfolio
		◯ Liquidity

TICKER

ENTRY	Execution Price	Where Did You Find The Trade	Purchase Date
WHY	What Indicators Confirmed The Trade		
EXIT	Stop Loss Price Level		Profit Target
WHY	Reason Sold		Date Sold

NOTES

	DATE	**RISK MANAGEMENT**
		◯ 1-2% of Your Portfolio ◯ Liquidity

TICKER

ENTRY	Execution Price	Where Did You Find The Trade	Purchase Date
WHY	What Indicators Confirmed The Trade		
EXIT	Stop Loss Price Level	Profit Target	
WHY	Reason Sold	Date Sold	

NOTES

	DATE	**RISK MANAGEMENT**
		○ 1-2% of Your Portfolio
		○ Liquidity

TICKER			
ENTRY	Execution Price	Where Did You Find The Trade	Purchase Date
WHY	What Indicators Confirmed The Trade		
EXIT	Stop Loss Price Level		Profit Target
WHY	Reason Sold		Date Sold

NOTES

_____
_____
_____
_____
_____
_____
_____
_____
_____

DATE	**RISK MANAGEMENT**
	○ 1-2% of Your Portfolio
	○ Liquidity

TICKER

ENTRY	Execution Price	Where Did You Find The Trade	Purchase Date
WHY	What Indicators Confirmed The Trade		
EXIT	Stop Loss Price Level		Profit Target
WHY	Reason Sold		Date Sold

NOTES

_____
_____
_____
_____
_____
_____
_____
_____
_____

DATE	RISK MANAGEMENT
	○ 1-2% of Your Portfolio
	○ Liquidity

TICKER

ENTRY

Execution Price	Where Did You Find The Trade	Purchase Date

WHY

What Indicators Confirmed The Trade

EXIT

Stop Loss Price Level	Profit Target

WHY

Reason Sold	Date Sold

NOTES

	DATE	**RISK MANAGEMENT**
		○ 1-2% of Your Portfolio
		○ Liquidity

TICKER

ENTRY	Execution Price	Where Did You Find The Trade	Purchase Date

WHY	What Indicators Confirmed The Trade

EXIT	Stop Loss Price Level	Profit Target

WHY	Reason Sold	Date Sold

NOTES

	DATE	**RISK MANAGEMENT**
		◯ 1-2% of Your Portfolio
		◯ Liquidity

TICKER

ENTRY	Execution Price	Where Did You Find The Trade	Purchase Date

WHY	What Indicators Confirmed The Trade

EXIT	Stop Loss Price Level	Profit Target

WHY	Reason Sold	Date Sold

NOTES

	DATE	**RISK MANAGEMENT**	
		◯ 1-2% of Your Portfolio	
		◯ Liquidity	

TICKER			
ENTRY	Execution Price	Where Did You Find The Trade	Purchase Date
WHY	What Indicators Confirmed The Trade		
EXIT	Stop Loss Price Level	Profit Target	
WHY	Reason Sold	Date Sold	

NOTES

DATE	RISK MANAGEMENT
	◯ 1-2% of Your Portfolio
	◯ Liquidity

TICKER

ENTRY

Execution Price	Where Did You Find The Trade	Purchase Date

WHY

What Indicators Confirmed The Trade

EXIT

Stop Loss Price Level	Profit Target

WHY

Reason Sold	Date Sold

NOTES

	DATE	**RISK MANAGEMENT**
		◯ 1-2% of Your Portfolio
		◯ Liquidity

TICKER

ENTRY	Execution Price	Where Did You Find The Trade	Purchase Date

WHY	What Indicators Confirmed The Trade

EXIT	Stop Loss Price Level	Profit Target

WHY	Reason Sold	Date Sold

NOTES

_____

_____

_____

_____

_____

_____

_____

_____

_____

DATE	RISK MANAGEMENT
	◯ 1-2% of Your Portfolio ◯ Liquidity

TICKER

ENTRY

Execution Price	Where Did You Find The Trade	Purchase Date

WHY

What Indicators Confirmed The Trade

EXIT

Stop Loss Price Level	Profit Target

WHY

Reason Sold	Date Sold

NOTES

_____
_____
_____
_____
_____
_____
_____
_____
_____

DATE	RISK MANAGEMENT
	○ 1-2% of Your Portfolio
	○ Liquidity

TICKER

ENTRY

Execution Price	Where Did You Find The Trade	Purchase Date

WHY

What Indicators Confirmed The Trade

EXIT

Stop Loss Price Level	Profit Target

WHY

Reason Sold	Date Sold

NOTES

_____
_____
_____
_____
_____
_____
_____
_____
_____

	DATE	RISK MANAGEMENT
		○ 1-2% of Your Portfolio
		○ Liquidity

TICKER

ENTRY	Execution Price	Where Did You Find The Trade	Purchase Date
WHY	What Indicators Confirmed The Trade		
EXIT	Stop Loss Price Level	Profit Target	
WHY	Reason Sold	Date Sold	

NOTES

DATE	RISK MANAGEMENT
	○ 1-2% of Your Portfolio
	○ Liquidity

TICKER

ENTRY

Execution Price	Where Did You Find The Trade	Purchase Date

WHY

What Indicators Confirmed The Trade

EXIT

Stop Loss Price Level	Profit Target

WHY

Reason Sold	Date Sold

NOTES

	DATE	**RISK MANAGEMENT**
		◯ 1-2% of Your Portfolio
		◯ Liquidity

TICKER			
ENTRY	Execution Price	Where Did You Find The Trade	Purchase Date
WHY	What Indicators Confirmed The Trade		
EXIT	Stop Loss Price Level	Profit Target	
WHY	Reason Sold	Date Sold	

NOTES

_____
_____
_____
_____
_____
_____
_____
_____

	DATE	**RISK MANAGEMENT**	
		◯ 1-2% of Your Portfolio ◯ Liquidity	

TICKER			
ENTRY	Execution Price	Where Did You Find The Trade	Purchase Date
WHY	What Indicators Confirmed The Trade		
EXIT	Stop Loss Price Level		Profit Target
WHY	Reason Sold		Date Sold

NOTES

	DATE	**RISK MANAGEMENT**
		○ 1-2% of Your Portfolio
		○ Liquidity

TICKER

ENTRY	Execution Price	Where Did You Find The Trade	Purchase Date
WHY	What Indicators Confirmed The Trade		
EXIT	Stop Loss Price Level		Profit Target
WHY	Reason Sold		Date Sold

NOTES

_____
_____
_____
_____
_____
_____
_____
_____
_____

	DATE	**RISK MANAGEMENT**
		◯ 1-2% of Your Portfolio
		◯ Liquidity

TICKER

ENTRY	Execution Price	Where Did You Find The Trade	Purchase Date
WHY	What Indicators Confirmed The Trade		
EXIT	Stop Loss Price Level		Profit Target
WHY	Reason Sold		Date Sold

NOTES

	DATE	RISK MANAGEMENT
		◯ 1-2% of Your Portfolio
		◯ Liquidity

TICKER

ENTRY	Execution Price	Where Did You Find The Trade	Purchase Date

WHY	What Indicators Confirmed The Trade

EXIT	Stop Loss Price Level	Profit Target

WHY	Reason Sold	Date Sold

NOTES

	DATE	**RISK MANAGEMENT**
		◯ 1-2% of Your Portfolio
		◯ Liquidity

TICKER			
ENTRY	Execution Price	Where Did You Find The Trade	Purchase Date
WHY	What Indicators Confirmed The Trade		
EXIT	Stop Loss Price Level		Profit Target
WHY	Reason Sold		Date Sold

NOTES

DATE	RISK MANAGEMENT
	◯ 1-2% of Your Portfolio
	◯ Liquidity

TICKER

ENTRY	Execution Price	Where Did You Find The Trade	Purchase Date

WHY	What Indicators Confirmed The Trade

EXIT	Stop Loss Price Level	Profit Target

WHY	Reason Sold	Date Sold

NOTES

DATE	RISK MANAGEMENT
	○ 1-2% of Your Portfolio
	○ Liquidity

TICKER

ENTRY

Execution Price	Where Did You Find The Trade	Purchase Date

WHY

What Indicators Confirmed The Trade

EXIT

Stop Loss Price Level	Profit Target

WHY

Reason Sold	Date Sold

NOTES

	DATE	**RISK MANAGEMENT**
		◯ 1-2% of Your Portfolio
		◯ Liquidity

TICKER

ENTRY	Execution Price	Where Did You Find The Trade	Purchase Date

WHY	What Indicators Confirmed The Trade

EXIT	Stop Loss Price Level	Profit Target

WHY	Reason Sold	Date Sold

NOTES

_____
_____
_____
_____
_____
_____
_____
_____
_____

	DATE	**RISK MANAGEMENT**
		◯ 1-2% of Your Portfolio
		◯ Liquidity

TICKER			
ENTRY	Execution Price	Where Did You Find The Trade	Purchase Date
WHY	What Indicators Confirmed The Trade		
EXIT	Stop Loss Price Level		Profit Target
WHY	Reason Sold		Date Sold

NOTES

DATE	RISK MANAGEMENT
	◯ 1-2% of Your Portfolio
	◯ Liquidity

TICKER

ENTRY

Execution Price	Where Did You Find The Trade	Purchase Date

WHY

What Indicators Confirmed The Trade

EXIT

Stop Loss Price Level	Profit Target

WHY

Reason Sold	Date Sold

NOTES

	DATE	RISK MANAGEMENT
		○ 1-2% of Your Portfolio
		○ Liquidity

TICKER

ENTRY	Execution Price	Where Did You Find The Trade	Purchase Date

WHY	What Indicators Confirmed The Trade

EXIT	Stop Loss Price Level	Profit Target

WHY	Reason Sold	Date Sold

NOTES

	DATE	**RISK MANAGEMENT**
		◯ 1-2% of Your Portfolio
		◯ Liquidity

TICKER

ENTRY	Execution Price	Where Did You Find The Trade	Purchase Date

WHY	What Indicators Confirmed The Trade

EXIT	Stop Loss Price Level	Profit Target

WHY	Reason Sold	Date Sold

NOTES

	DATE	**RISK MANAGEMENT**
		◯ 1-2% of Your Portfolio
		◯ Liquidity

TICKER

ENTRY	Execution Price	Where Did You Find The Trade	Purchase Date

WHY	What Indicators Confirmed The Trade

EXIT	Stop Loss Price Level	Profit Target

WHY	Reason Sold	Date Sold

NOTES

	DATE	RISK MANAGEMENT
		○ 1-2% of Your Portfolio
		○ Liquidity

TICKER

ENTRY	Execution Price	Where Did You Find The Trade	Purchase Date
WHY	What Indicators Confirmed The Trade		
EXIT	Stop Loss Price Level	Profit Target	
WHY	Reason Sold	Date Sold	

NOTES

DATE	RISK MANAGEMENT
	○ 1-2% of Your Portfolio ○ Liquidity

TICKER

ENTRY	Execution Price	Where Did You Find The Trade	Purchase Date

WHY	What Indicators Confirmed The Trade

EXIT	Stop Loss Price Level	Profit Target

WHY	Reason Sold	Date Sold

NOTES

	DATE	**RISK MANAGEMENT**
		◯ 1-2% of Your Portfolio
		◯ Liquidity

TICKER

ENTRY	Execution Price	Where Did You Find The Trade	Purchase Date
WHY	What Indicators Confirmed The Trade		
EXIT	Stop Loss Price Level		Profit Target
WHY	Reason Sold		Date Sold

NOTES

___
___
___
___
___
___
___
___

DATE	RISK MANAGEMENT
	○ 1-2% of Your Portfolio ○ Liquidity

TICKER

ENTRY

Execution Price	Where Did You Find The Trade	Purchase Date

WHY

What Indicators Confirmed The Trade

EXIT

Stop Loss Price Level	Profit Target

WHY

Reason Sold	Date Sold

NOTES

DATE	RISK MANAGEMENT
	○ 1-2% of Your Portfolio
	○ Liquidity

TICKER

ENTRY	Execution Price	Where Did You Find The Trade	Purchase Date
WHY	What Indicators Confirmed The Trade		
EXIT	Stop Loss Price Level		Profit Target
WHY	Reason Sold		Date Sold

NOTES

	DATE	**RISK MANAGEMENT**
		◯ 1-2% of Your Portfolio
		◯ Liquidity

TICKER

ENTRY

Execution Price	Where Did You Find The Trade	Purchase Date

WHY

What Indicators Confirmed The Trade

EXIT

Stop Loss Price Level	Profit Target

WHY

Reason Sold	Date Sold

NOTES

DATE	**RISK MANAGEMENT**
	◯ 1-2% of Your Portfolio
	◯ Liquidity

TICKER

ENTRY

Execution Price	Where Did You Find The Trade	Purchase Date

WHY

What Indicators Confirmed The Trade

EXIT

Stop Loss Price Level	Profit Target

WHY

Reason Sold	Date Sold

NOTES

_____
_____
_____
_____
_____
_____
_____
_____
_____

	DATE	**RISK MANAGEMENT**
		◯ 1-2% of Your Portfolio
		◯ Liquidity

TICKER

ENTRY

Execution Price	Where Did You Find The Trade	Purchase Date

WHY

What Indicators Confirmed The Trade

EXIT

Stop Loss Price Level	Profit Target

WHY

Reason Sold	Date Sold

NOTES

DATE	RISK MANAGEMENT
	◯ 1-2% of Your Portfolio
	◯ Liquidity

TICKER

ENTRY	Execution Price	Where Did You Find The Trade	Purchase Date

WHY	What Indicators Confirmed The Trade

EXIT	Stop Loss Price Level	Profit Target

WHY	Reason Sold	Date Sold

NOTES

Made in the USA
Middletown, DE
24 July 2020